Discovering
in the Body of Christ

Discovering Your Place in the Body of Christ

Selwyn Hughes

Marshall Pickering

Marshall Pickering
Marshall Morgan & Scott
34–42 Cleveland Street, London, W1P 5FB

Copyright © Selwyn Hughes 1982
First Published by Marshall Morgan & Scott 1982

This re-issue published in 1989 by
Marshall Morgan & Scott Publications Ltd,
Part of the Marshall Pickering Holdings Group

ISBN 0 551 00946 2

Printed in Great Britain by
Cox & Wyman Ltd,
Reading, Berkshire

Contents

Preface

The books in the *Christian Counselling Series* are written with two main groups of people in mind. The first group are those who facing a personal problem look for something concise and readable that speaks to their need. The second group are ministers and counsellors who wish to place in the hands of people seeking help something that will supplement their own individual counselling efforts.

The authors, writing from their own personal encounters with people who have faced the problems listed in this series, do so with a good deal of confidence. They claim that when the principles outlined in these books have been followed they have contributed in a positive manner to helping people resolve their difficulties. The content is firmly based on Scripture, but the authors in their writing seek to apply Biblical principles in such a way that helps readers, not only to know what they should do but how to do it.

1

What is the Church?

'I just don't know what to do. I've been a Christian for less than a year and I've been given a job in my church which is getting me down. Everyone thinks I am well fitted for the task they have given me but I know deep down in my heart it is not the place God has for me. I'm afraid I will have to give up going to church unless someone tries to understand my problem and help me.'

Brian, a 25 year old accountant, came for counselling because he had been assigned a task by the officials of his local church which he felt was not in line with his basic spiritual abilities. As a result he was experiencing a good deal of anxiety and frustration. After several hours of counselling, during which he was shown how to discover and develop his basic spiritual gift, he returned to his church and suggested to his minister that he be given a task more in harmony with the basic gifts God had given him. After long discussion with the minister and the elders, when Brian was able to share the results of his counselling session with me, he convinced the church leadership that the role they expected him to play in the growth of the church was incompatible with his natural spiritual abilities. Brian was then given a new task: one more in harmony with his basic gifts and which gave him a great degree of spiritual fulfilment.

The minister of the church, when writing to me a little later concerning Brian's situation, said, 'We have decided to approach every member of our church in a much more cautious and prayerful manner than we have previously done so that we help them to discover, not what we want them to be doing but rather what are God's purposes for their lives in this part of His Body, the Church'.

How sad it is that in many churches people are assigned tasks for which they are not fitted either by natural or spiritual endowment and they become, so to speak, like square pegs in round holes. The subject of discovering our proper place in the Body of Christ, although well understood and practised by the Early Church, is greatly neglected by Christians here in the Twentieth Century. It is my conviction that a Christian who discovers and develops his basic spiritual gift will function in the Body of Christ with *maximum effectiveness and minimum weariness*. If he fails to discover the place God wants him to fulfil and tries to undertake a task for which he is not divinely fitted, then he will function in that role with *minimum effectiveness and maximum weariness*.

10

Paul, the great planter and builder of New Testament churches took care to teach his converts the principle of discovering their basic gifts as one of life's priorities. His desire for every newly formed church was that they might develop their ministries in harmony with God's personal plan for their lives. Take, for example, the situation in the New Testament churches mentioned in Acts 14.1–18. These churches, being newly formed, had no members mature enough to qualify as elders or deacons, but thrown on the inner resources provided by the Holy Spirit, no doubt they put into practice Paul's teaching on the discovery and development of their gifts so that within a comparatively short time the members had matured enough for some to be chosen as elders on Paul's return visit. (See Acts 14.21–23). You see, in every congregation of God's people the the basic gifts needed for the development and maturity of that group are already deposited there by God. The task left to us is to discover these gifts, develop them and use them in the way God desires.

Before we can begin to discover and develop our basic spiritual abilities, however, we must first comprehend the *nature* of Christ's church. As a first-hand observer of the spiritual life of the church for over 35 years, I have come to the conclusion that the Christian church is suffering from an identity crisis. It's like an amnesia victim trying to find out 'Who am I?' We are divided by so many different ideas, doctrines and denominations that we are in danger of losing our proper spiritual identity.

What then is the Church of Jesus Christ? Is it something tall and Gothic, with beautiful architecture and stained glass windows? No, that is the house in which the Church worships. The Church is people – born again people. They may meet in a Cathedral or in a cottage; a magnificent complex, or an ordinary house; but the building is relatively unimportant. 'The Church' said someone, 'is a farmer ploughing in the field, a housewife at the kitchen sink, a mechanic in a garage, a student in a classroom. Wherever there is a heart that is redeemed by the Blood of Jesus Christ, there the Church exists.'

The Apostle Paul's favourite analogy of the Church in both Corinthians and Ephesians, is the body. It throbs with life: Jesus Christ is its head and you and I, as believers, are its members. The members are gifted to function as an organism and they have a rich fellowship with one another. Every single believer is like a living cell in that body, and for the body to function effectively every cell must live in harmony with all the other cells.

Wherever a group of those living cells of Christ's Body meet to organise themselves into a community for fellowship and spiritual enrichment, there a local church exists. The New Testament gives specific instructions on how a local church should

12

function and pays a good deal of attention to the principles underlying the corporate functioning of such a group of God's people. The question is often asked, however: 'What defines a local church? When does a group of God's people meeting together become a church?'

Throughout history many have tried to define what constitutes a local church and their efforts have served us well. The Reformers, for instance, gave the following definition: 'The Church exists where the Word of God is preached and where the sacraments of Baptism and Holy Communion are faithfully administered: to the end that men would come to faith in Christ.' Some of the Reformers also included a statement that the exercise of church discipline was necessary in order for a local church to be a bona fide part of the Body of Christ.

Rome countered this definition with one of her own which is roughly as follows: 'The Church is made up of the faithful baptised who receive the sacraments under the government of the priesthood who, in turn, are under the authority of one visible head on earth.' Others have attempted to define the Church in terms of style of living and code of behaviour. Some local churches, as well as denominations, define true believers in terms of specific things they do, and certain things they don't do. These definitions include such things as the use of money, wearing of jewelry, types of dress, modes of entertainment, and so on.

Francis Schaeffer indicates seven ingredients
which he claims must be part of 'the policy of the
church as a church'

1. Local congregations made up of Christians
2. Special meetings on the first day of the week
3. Church officers (elders) who have responsibility for the local churches
4. Deacons responsible for the community of the
   church in the area of material things
5. A serious view of church discipline
6. Specific qualifications for elders and deacons
7. The observance of two sacraments, baptism
   and the Lord's Supper.

A good deal could be written on the subject of the
nature of the universal church and the local church
but that is not the primary purpose of this booklet.

The way I would answer the question: 'What constitutes a local church?' is like this: 'A local church
exists whenever a company of believers meet
together around the Word of God, submit to its
authority and are organised under the leadership of
a properly constituted governing body that exer-
cises Scriptural disciplines and control to the end of
bringing Christians to maturity and non Christians
into a personal relationship with Jesus Christ.' This
I believe to be the irreducible minimum for a local
church run on New Testament principles.

In order for a local church to develop spiritual

14

maturity all of its members must function in the way God designed them. Paul puts it like this: 'Now here is what I am trying to say: All of you together are the one Body of Christ and each one of you is a separate and necessary part of it.' (1 Cor. 12.27 TLB). As in the human body each part is designed to function in harmony and interdependence, so are we positioned in Christ's Body to perform a specific and God-designed task. *Performing that task to the fullest possible degree is the main calling of every Christian.*

It becomes clear when we read the New Testament that God does not expect any believer to live in isolation. In Matthew 18.19 Jesus said that if two Christians agree on earth concerning anything they ask, his Father in heaven will do it. He went on to say (verse 20) 'For where two or three gather because they are mine, I will be right there among them.' (TLB) Paul, writing to the Romans says, 'Just as there are many parts to our bodies, so it is with Christ's body. We are all parts of it, and it takes every one of us to make it complete, for we each have different work to do. So we belong to each and each needs all the others' (Romans 12.4–5 TLB).

For Christ's Body to be in perfect health all of its members must function as they have been designed. Each believer must see that he or she is in the Body, not primarily to express themselves but to build up the Body. A cancerous cell, so I am told, is one that ceases to be contributive and seeks not to minister, but to be ministered unto. Once a cell in our bodies ceases to become contributive then it can become cancerous. Once we understand that our place in Christ's Body is to minister to the needs of others and not to get others to minister to our needs we are on the way to true fulfilment, for fulfilment comes not through getting but through giving.

One of the reasons for frustration amongst believers arises from the fact that they do not know precisely what it is God has fitted them to do in His Body. Joy comes when we discover our place in the Body of Christ, fit into the perfect pattern that God has prepared for us and contribute to the functioning of Christ's Church according to God's design. Every Christian has at least one basic gift. You may feel very inept and inadequate, but believe me God has gifted you to do at least one thing well in the community of believers we call the Church. So congratulations – you're gifted! Sometimes ministers unwittingly curb the development of gifts within a congregation when they play the 'I've-got-to-do-everything' role. Where this happens spiritual gifts lie dormant in the lives of those who form that particular congregation, when really they should be taking an active part in the ministries of teaching, counselling, etc. The frozen assets of the Church will never be thawed out until we put into practice the Biblical doctrine of discovering our basic gifts. Then, and only then, will unemployment be rooted out from amongst God's people and the universal priesthood of all believers truly realised.

2

Basic gifts – gifts we have

The New Testament introduces us to three distinct streams of gifts which are listed respectively in Romans 12.6–8, 1 Corinthians 12.8–10 and Ephesians 4.11–12. After studying these passages for a number of years now it is my belief that each member of the Trinity assumes responsibility for the administration and operation of a particular set of gifts. In Ephesians 4.11–12 the gifts there are described as coming under the direct control of our Lord Jesus Christ. In other words they are Christ's gifts to His Church. In 1 Corinthians 12.8–10 the gifts are said to be under the control and administration of the Holy Spirit. In Romans 12, although there is no specific reference to these gifts coming under the direct control and administration of the Father, I believe it safe to assume, on the basis of what I have said, and considering the precise nature of these gifts, that they are distributed and administered by God the Father. The gifts outlined in Romans 12 for the purpose of this study will be

19

described as 'basic gifts'.

Before we begin to examine the first list of gifts in detail we must pause to clarify the difference between a basic gift and a talent. Simply defined a basic gift is a spiritual motivation or an inward drive within our personalities which prompts us to minister in certain directions within the Body of Christ. A talent is a natural aptitude to do something well, such as an ability to paint, to sing, to write, to speak, and so on.

According to the Scriptures, before we were born, God's sovereignty was at work preparing us for our emergence into this world. The Psalmist said 'You were there while I was being formed in utter seclusion! You saw me before I was born and scheduled each day of my life before I began to breathe. Every day was recorded in your book' (Psalm 139:15–16 TLB). God shaped Jeremiah for his ministry saying to him, 'Before I formed you in the womb I knew you and before you were born I consecrated you' (Jeremiah 1:5) According to these and other Scriptures (see Luke 1:16, Galatians 1:15) a Sovereign God is at work preparing us to contribute to His universe in certain well defined ways. In each one of us God builds into our personalities at the moment of conception (so I believe) certain aptitudes and abilities which later, through growth and development become observable. Once we become Christians however, a spiritual transformation takes place in which the Holy Spirit regenerates our dead human spirits (See Ephesians 2:1) and brings us to new life and a new identity. Immediately we are converted at least one of our basic abilities (sometimes more than one) is harnessed by the Holy Spirit to become our specific contribution to the ministry of development in Christ's Body, the Church. There takes place within us, whether we feel it or not an inner thrust, or if you like, a distinct motivation which leads us toward a specific form of ministry in Christ's Body. This inner drive is what constitutes a basic gift. It is the heightening and intensification, or as some prefer to call it, the 'Christianising' of a natural ability in such a way that an individual finds himself inwardly motivated to play a certain part in building up the Church.

A basic gift then is a spiritual urge or motivation, produced by the Holy Spirit alighting and impinging on a natural ability so as to sanctify it, and transfigure it that it becomes the potential for a significant contribution in the ministry of the Church. It does not mean that every natural ability is taken up by God in this way but one at least, most certainly is, enabling believers to play their part in the most wonderful ministry in the universe – maintaining the health and vitality of Christ's Church here on earth.

It is my belief that every Christian has at least one basic gift and is specifically called by God to contribute to His Church in a certain way. Without that gift then no positive contribution can be made to Christ's Body because the Church is a spiritual organism, not a natural one, and requires for its growth and enlargement, a spiritual input. In order to be able to understand what part we are designed to play in Christ's Body, we must examine the set of gifts described in Romans 12 in detail: 'Through the grace of God we have different gifts. If our gift is preaching, let us preach to the limit of our vision. If it is serving others, let us concentrate on our service. If it is teaching, let us give all we have to our teaching: and if our gift be the stimulating of the faith of others, let us set ourselves to it. Let the man who is called to give, give freely; let the man who wields authority think of his responsibility, and let the man who feels sympathy for his fellows act cheerfully.' (J. B. Phillips). It can be seen from this that there are seven specific gifts mentioned here:

1. *Preaching:* The Greek word used here is *propheteia* which means public exposition or presenting truth with force, clarity and conviction. Some translations use the word 'prophecy' here but this use of the word is not the same as the gift of prophecy spoken of in 1 Corinthians 12, or the office of a prophet as described in Ephesians 4.11. It is the gift of inspired preaching; the God-given ability to present truth in such a way that it touches

the conscience of the hearers and exposes unrighteous motives.

2. *Serving:* This is a gift which enables the recipient to be extremely sensitive to the personal needs of others. A person who has this gift will demonstrate a deep concern and desire to help another brother or sister in practical ways so that they can be freed for greater and more effective service. Such a person also will overlook personal comfort and convenience so that the needs of others can be met.

3. *Teaching:* This gift enables the one who possesses it to clarify Biblical truth with great effectiveness. Such a person will find within himself a deep desire to search out and validate truth, dig around for important facts, manifest great diligence in study and compare one Scripture with another so that the truth can be presented in a proper perspective.

4. *Stimulating the faith of others:* This, I believe, is the gift of personal counselling. Some people in Christ's Body are gifted with spiritual eagerness to help others with their problems. Whenever they see a weak or lame Christian something rises within them to respond by personal encouragement and counselling. They have that special ability to come alongside a struggling believer, to say the right words and to minister to them in such a way that helps them resolve their problems.

5. *Giving:* A person with this gift will manifest a

23

high degree of wisdom in relation to material giving. Such a person will show skill in organising their personal affairs and assets so as to be able to enrich the work of God in material ways. The gift carries within it a God-given wisdom to make quick and sound decisions about the right use of money.

6. *Wielding Authority:* A person with this gift will show a great ability to preside over the activities of others and be able to co-ordinate other people's labour and activities toward the best advantage. Such a person will not only be able to look ahead and distinguish major objectives for the group or the community, but will also have the ability to clarify them for others.

7. *Sympathy:* √This gift enables a person to demonstrate a deep sympathy and empathic understanding toward the misfortune of others. Such a person will find it easy to enter into the emotional needs of others and relate to them in a helpful way. There will be a warmth flowing from them that can bring healing to the one who is downcast, without any words being spoken.

Someone has described these gifts as 'an inward drive which comes to life at conversion by which we contribute to the health and growth of His Body, the Church.' Some will be motivated to preach, others to teach, others to stimulate the faith of those who are weak by coming alongside them with helpful advice and encouragement. Some will find

24

themselves motivated perhaps in two or three directions. In addition to the gift of inspired preaching, for example, they might find themselves motivated to co-ordinate the activities of others – the gift of ruling or administration. And they might even find themselves motivated also in the direction of stimulating the faith of others.

What we must realise is that every Christian has at least one of these gifts, probably more than one, and it is only when we discover this gift (or gifts) and begin to develop it (them) that we can experience true fulfilment in the Body of Christ. I said earlier that one of the main reasons for frustration amongst believers arises from the fact that many do not rightly understand their basic ministry in the Body of Christ. Joy and fulfilment come however when we discover our basic gift and exercise it in the way God has planned.

What happens if we fail to discover and develop our basic spiritual gift? Several things can take place: (1) *We become jealous and envious of the ministry of others*. We look at people who are functioning in the way they were designed to function, see their happiness and fulfilment and say to ourselves: 'Why can't I be like them?' We forget, however, that joy comes not through copying others but by doing the thing that God has designed us to achieve. (2) *We become anxious and insecure*. Nothing contributes to anxiety and insecurity more than the belief 'I am

25

not sure what God wants me to do.' Once we are properly engaged in doing what God planned us to do then anxiety and insecurity drop away as the leaves fall from the trees in the autumn. (3) *We become critical and judgmental in our attitudes.* Many Christians go about criticising the work of others in the Body of Christ because they feel unfulfilled in themselves. Psychology has shown us that a critical attitude often stems from a feeling of deprivation and unhappiness. We don't feel of much use ourselves and we try to compensate for it by condemning and criticising others. Once we have a positive understanding of our place in Christ's Body and the function He has called us to fulfill we give no room for jealousy, insecurity, or a spirit of criticism to arise within our hearts.

Permit me, at this stage, to share with you a personal experience. I was converted to Christ at the age of 15 and after I had been a Christian for about three years a group of friends approached me and told me that, in their opinion, I had within me the gift of a Pastor. 'We can see it quite clearly,' they said 'and we think you ought to go to a theological college and train for the ministry'. I thanked them for their advice and at once wrote off to a theological college and was accepted as a candidate for the ministry. After leaving college I settled in several pastorates, all of which were greatly blessed by God. Congregations grew in numbers, the church finances increased and my friends and colleagues told me that I was a highly successful pastor. What they didn't know, however, was that inside I was deeply unhappy and greatly frustrated.

This inner frustration led in due course to a serious breakdown in my health. In fact at one point my doctors reported to my wife that they were unable to diagnose my sickness and if something dramatic did not take place within two or three days I would be dead. Well, something dramatic did take place. One evening whilst reading John 10.10 God broke in on my piteous condition and within a matter of minutes restored me to complete physical health. It was a miracle – one that my wife, doctors and friends joyously recognised. Following that dramatic healing I began to re-evaluate my ministry in terms of what God had fitted me to do, not so much what others thought I ought to be doing. It was during this time of re-appraisal that I discovered the relevance of the three streams of gifts I have already referred to, and I began to ask myself some searching questions: 'Am I really a pastor?' 'Is this the ministry God has for me or has He designed me for some other purpose?' I laid aside all my preconceived ideas and came like a little child to the holy fountain of Scripture. For days I pondered and prayed over the three streams of gifts until the concept I am now sharing with you began to dawn upon me.

I saw that the first stream of gifts were gifts that we are given at our conversion, or implanted in our spirit before we were even created. My task now was to find out which of those gifts I possessed. But what about the second and third streams of gifts? What place or purpose did these have in my life? I came to realise that the gifts of the Spirit described in 1 Corinthians 12 were gifts that we are encouraged to *seek*: they are given to us as we open ourselves to the ministry of the Holy Spirit in accordance with God's sovereign purpose for our lives. The third stream of gifts, the gifts of Christ, outlined in Ephesians 4, were neither gifts we have nor gifts we should seek, but gifts we *become*. Not all Christians become pastors, teachers, evangelists, apostles, prophets: indeed only a small minority are chosen by Christ for these ministries in His Body. I saw that my problem had been that I had started out to become a pastor instead of first recognising my basic gift and then proceeding to build from there. Once I discovered and began to develop my basic gifts and sought the gifts of the Spirit that best amplified and extended my basic gifts, I found that with no pushing or aspiration on my part, my ministry developed into that of a teacher and an evangelist. *This was confirmed by several church leaders* who witnessed in their own spirits that this was the ministry I had been designed by God to pursue.

I then resigned from the pastorate and began to

pursue the ministries God had equipped me to perform. Almost immediately I discovered that I was achieving more in the Kingdom of God by doing less. Instead of minimum effectiveness with maximum weariness, it was now maximum effectiveness with minimum weariness. I had found my niche in the Body of Christ – and what a wonderful release came with this discovery.

Now I can almost hear you say: 'How do I go about discovering my basic gifts? What exactly do I need to do in order to find the niche God has prepared for me?' This is the subject of the next chapter.

3

A chart to help you discover your basic gift

Before we focus on a simple but practical exercise to help us identify our basic gift or gifts, here are some important points to consider: 1. *Acquaint yourself with the meaning and purpose of each of the seven basic gifts*. Go over the list of basic gifts in chapter 2 once again until you are sure you understand the meaning and function of each one. A jeweller who wants to deal in diamonds must acquaint himself with all kinds of gems. You will be able to identify your own gift or gifts much more easily if you take time to examine and understand each one.

2. *Approach the issue in a spirit of prayer and dedication*. When you consider that Paul's listing of the seven basic gifts in Romans 12 follows hard on the heels of his earnest appeal for every Christian to 'present your bodies as a living sacrifice' it suggests we ought to approach the whole subject in an attitude of prayerful expectancy. Dedication always precedes revelation. When you dedicate your body

to God as a living sacrifice then you will discover where you fit into His Body.

3. *Recognize that the following practical guide to discovering your basic gift is simply a tool and must not be over-rated*. As you follow the instructions on the next page keep in mind that the statements together with the chart are designed to focus on the inner motivation of your spirit, or the inner drive that God has given you to function in a certain way within His body. Such an important spiritual exercise needs further confirmation by those in your local church or fellowship. In fact, other Christians often see a gift in us long before we ourselves are aware of it. Discuss the outcome with other believers, particularly with those who know you well and who are mature Christians.

ALL GOD'S CHILDREN HAVE GIFTS

1. I enjoy presenting God's truth in an inspired and enthusiastic way. 2   2
2. I am always ready to overlook my own personal comfort in order that the needs of others may be met. 3   2
3. I find great delight in explaining the truth of a text within its context. 1   3
4. I am able to verbally encourage those who waver and are spiritually troubled. 2 3

5. I am able to manage my financial affairs efficiently so that I can give generously to the Lord's work. 3

1 1

6. I find it easy to delegate responsibility and organise others towards spiritual achievement. 0

2

7. I readily find myself sympathising with the misfortunes of others. 3

2

8. I am conscious of a persuasiveness of speech when encouraging people to examine their spiritual motives. 1

1

9. I have the knack of making people feel at home. 2

3

10. I delight in digging out facts concerning the Bible so that I can pass them on to others. 0

2

11. I have a deep concern to encourage people toward spiritual growth and achievement. 0

1

12. I am cheerful about giving material assets so that the Lord's work can be furthered. 3

2

13. I am able to effectively supervise the activities of others. 0

1

14. I enjoy visiting those in hospital, or the shut in's. 2

0

15. I am able to present the Word of God to a congregation of people with clarity, and conviction. 1

2

16. I am happy when asked to assist others in the Lord's work, without necessarily being appointed to a leadership position. 3

2

17. I am concerned that truth should be presented in a clear fashion with proper attention to the meaning of words. 1

3

18. I am at my best when treating those who are spiritually wounded. / 1 2
19. I have no problem in joyfully entrusting my assets to others for the work of the ministry. 2 2
20. I am able to plan the actions of others with ease and supply them with details which will enable them to work effectively. 0 2
21. I have a great concern for those involved in trouble. 2 1
22. I find myself preaching for a verdict whenever I present the truths of the Word of God. 2 1
23. I delight in providing a gracious haven for guests. 2 2
24. I am diligent in my study of the Bible and give careful attention to necessary research. 0 2
25. I am able to help those who need counselling over personal problems. 1 2
26. I am concerned over the question of financial assistance being available for all sections of the church. 2 1
27. I am deeply sensitive to the need of a smooth running administration so that every phase of activity is carried out decently and in order. 0 1
28. I work happily with those who are ignored by the majority. 2 2
29. I find my preaching brings people to a definite point of decision. 1 2
30. I enjoy taking the load from key people so that they can put more effort into their own particular task. 1 1

34

31. I am able to explain well how the Bible hangs together. 2   ·2

32. I am acutely aware of the things that hold people back in their spiritual development and long to help them overcome their problems.   2   1

33. I am careful with money and continually pray over its proper distribution in the work of the Lord.   3 / 1   1

34. I know where I am going and am able to take others with me.   1   2

35. I am able to relate to others emotionally and am quick to help when help is needed.   2   2

INSTRUCTIONS

Above are 35 statements which may help you discover your basic gift or gifts. Rate yourself with the following scale by writing the appropriate number in the corresponding number square. Ask yourself 'Is this statement true in my spiritual life and experience?' Then indicate your score in the appropriate number square on the following scale.

Greatly	3	Little	1
Some	2	Not at all	

After you have completed the test by rating yourself for each of the 35 statements, add the scores in each horizontal row. Record the number in the Total column. Your total score for each row indicates your level of interest in that particular gift. The highest scores may lead you to a clearer understanding of the basic spiritual gift or gifts which God has deposited in your life. After you have completed the test fill in the name of each gift in the appropriate column.

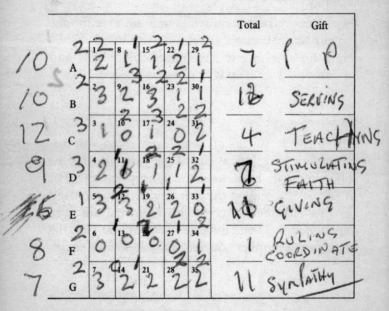

	1	2	3	4	5	Total	Gift
A	1 · 2	8 · 1	15 · 1	22 · 2	29 · 1	7	P
B	2 · 3	9 · 2	16 · 3	23 · 2	30 · 2	12	SERVING
C	3 · 1	10 · 0	17 · 3	24 · 0	31 · 2	4	TEACHING
D	4 · 2	11 · 0	18 · 1	25 · 1	32 · 2	7	STIMULATING FAITH
E	5 · 3	12 · 3	19 · 2	26 · 2	33 · 0	10	GIVING
F	6 · 0	13 · 0	20 · 0	27 · 0	34 · 1	1	RULING COORDINATE
G	7 · 3	14 · 2	21 · 2	28 · 2	35 · 2	11	SYMPATHY

(handwritten left margin: 10, 10, 12, 9, 16, 8, 7)

KEY TO YOUR SPIRITUAL GIFT

Row A – Prophecy; Row B – Serving; Row C – Teaching; Row D – Stimulating the faith of others; Row E – Giving; Row F – Ruling or Co-ordinating; Row G – Sympathy.

(handwritten: PROPHETIC SERVING TEACHING STIMULATE FAITH)

Here are some additional thoughts which will help you keep the matter of discovering your basic gift in proper perspective.

The absence of any particular gift in our lives does not excuse us from obedience to clear Scriptural commands. If, for example, a person discovers he does not have the gift of 'giving', he is still expected to support the Lord's work by his finances. Similarly, if a Christian finds he does not possess the gift of 'sympathy' he is still expected to 'show mercy and comfort the feeble minded' (1 Thess. 5.14). This may raise the question in your mind: 'If we are all expected to do these things then why the need for a specific gift?' The way I can best answer that question is like this: picture the Church as a football team. Every player in the team has a specific function but all are expected to try and get a goal. Each one of us has a commitment to live for Christ and to minister to each other in every way we possibly can, but God has gifted each one of us with special spiritual abilities in certain direction. This means that the enabling ministries of the Body are guaranteed and are not left to mere natural inclination. We should be watchful that the absence of a spiritual gift does not lead us into lethargy or an avoidance of our overall spiritual responsibilities.

Some Christians find it difficult to differentiate between 'gifts' and 'fruit' – spoken of in Galatians 5: I have often heard Christians refer to the nine qualities of the Fruit of the Spirit as 'gifts'. They say, 'I am praying for the gift of peace, or the gift of joy, or the gift of love.' The fruit of the Spirit is not a gift, but the result of abiding in Christ. As our roots go down deeply into Him and we live in fellowship with Him and His Word then the fruit of the Spirit will appear in our lives by direct consequence. Every one of the fruit of the Spirit ought to be seen in our lives and every Christian can and should have all nine qualities of the fruit of the Spirit. Gifts, however, are distributed by the prerogative of God and one person does not possess all the gifts. To help you differentiate between 'gifts' and 'fruit' keep in mind that fruit has to do with character and gifts have to do with service.

Our natural abilities and aptitudes (as mentioned earlier) are often a clue to the basic spiritual gifts resident within us. John Stott in one of his books makes the point that the Almighty is both the God of Creation and the God of Redemption. The God Who chose us before the foundation of the world (Ephesians 1.4–5) and Who prepared beforehand good works for us to walk in (Ephesians 2.10) is also God of Redemption Who pours His grace upon us and endows us with spiritual gifts. (Ephesians 4.7–11).

God has been sovereignly at work in our lives from the moment of conception and built into us certain abilities which He foreknew would equip us for ministry within His Body following our conversion. It stands to reason therefore that these abilities will show themselves in natural ways prior to our conversion, and after conversion become heightened and intensified to such a degree that they function in a much higher realm.

Gifts always make room for themselves. Once you discover that you have a basic gift, don't go around telling everyone, but adopt the attitude described by Paul in Philippians 2.3 'Don't be selfish; don't live to make a good impression on others. Be humble, thinking of others better than yourself. Don't just think about your own affairs, but be interested in others too, and in what they are doing' (TLB). Although your local church or fellowship may not at first recognise your basic gift, keep humble and prayerful and it will eventually make room for itself. The great preacher and Bible expositor of a previous generation, G. Campbell-Morgan, was rejected as a candidate for the ministry when he was 25, but his gifts eventually made room for him and he won world-wide recognition as a pastor, author and Bible teacher.

It is possible for a Christian to live for years, even a lifetime without a consciousness of being in possession of particular basic gifts. Unused gifts really squander the grace of God. This makes the need for discovery of our basic gifts one of the most vital subjects in the Church at this present moment.

Great joy flows through our lives when we exercise our basic gifts. The inner joy a person experiences in exercising a particular gift is often a clue as to its presence.

The delight and joy a person feels when ministering to others through a particular gift is communicated to those on the receiving end of that ministry and this is often reciprocated to the one ministering. This reciprocation then increases the measure of joy.

In the light of what we have said, does it not become imperative that every Christian in Christ's Body set about the task of attempting to discover and develop their basic spiritual gifts? It is only when we discover our basic gifts and seek to express them in Christ's Church that we can truly *build up* His Body.

4

The gifts of the Holy Spirit – gifts we seek

In 1 Corinthians 12.8–11 the Scripture records another set of gifts – nine in all – which are often referred to as the 'Nine Gifts of the Spirit'. Since the rise of the 'Charismatic Movement' it has become popular to describe these gifts as 'charismatic gifts', the thought being that unless one operates one or more of these special gifts then one is not 'charismatic'. The word *charisma* is derived from the Greek word *charis* which means 'grace'. The result of God's grace is a spiritual gift – *charisma*. In the plural form the word is *charismata* meaning the differing results of grace. Paul uses the word in his list of basic gifts in Romans 12.6: 'Since we have *charismata* that differ according to the *charis* given to us . . .' The word is used again in 1 Peter 4.10 where the apostle says 'As each has received a charisma employ it . . . as good stewards of the manifold *charis* of God'. To use the word 'charismatic' of a select group of Christians is Scripturally incorrect for in the Bible sense of the word *all Christ-*

41

ians are charismatic, as all have at least one gift.

In verse 1 of this chapter Paul uses the word *pneumatikoi* to describe the gifts. Although usually translated, 'spiritual gifts' a more literal translation of the word would be 'spiritual things' or 'spirituals'. The Greek word gives the thought of Spirit-endowed. These gifts are given and administered by the Holy Spirit for supernatural purposes and are not the result of training, experience, human insight, or prowess. If we eliminate the miraculous element from these gifts then we will miss completely the special part and place they have to play in the growth and development of Christ's Body.

Let us now proceed to examine them one by one and in the order in which they appear in the *Authorised Version*, the translation which, in my opinion, best brings out the truth of the Greek text:

Word of wisdom: This is not a gift of 'wisdom' in a general sense, but a supernatural impartation of a fragment of God's wisdom conveyed to the mind of a believer in a crisis situation. It functions in order to enable a Christian to solve deep and complex problems which are beyond one's natural ability to solve.

Word of knowledge: Notice again it is not a gift of knowledge but a word of knowledge. This gift operates when God drops into a person's mind a fragment of His knowledge given supernaturally for a temporary and specific purpose. A classic illustra-

tion of this gift is found in Acts 5 when Peter con-
fronted Ananaias and Sapphira with the fact that
they had kept back part of the purchase price of the
land which they had sold. Peter had no way of
knowing this apart from the knowledge which was
imparted to him by the Holy Spirit. This knowledge was something he could not have gained by
natural deduction but was imparted to him supernaturally by the Holy Spirit.

Faith: The Bible talks about saving faith
(Ephesians 2.8–9) and many other kinds of faith,
but the faith described here is *supernatural* faith –
the Divinely imparted ability to believe God in an
extremely difficult and perhaps dangerous situation. When it functions all human doubt is instantly
dissolved and the person operating this gift speaks
or acts in such a way that allows for no possible
miscarriage or failure. It is, in fact, God's faith,
dropped into the heart of a believer, enabling him to
speak and act in absolute confidence that what he
believes will come to pass.

The gifts of healing: The gifts of healing is the
supernatural ability to bring healing to others in the
power of the Holy Spirit. Notice the word here is in
the plural – *gifts* of healing. This indicates that some
Christians will demonstrate a gift for the healing of
certain kinds of sicknesses but not for others. In my
own experience, based on over thirty years in the
ministry of healing, I have discovered that certain

43

types of sicknesses and diseases respond more immediately to my own ministry of laying on of hands than do others.

The working of miracles: This again is a supernatural ability given by the Holy Spirit enabling a person to perform miraculous feats. It is the releasing of the creative power of God into a dark, difficult and serious situation. I believe an example of this is seen in Acts 13.1–12 where Paul demonstrated the power to bring blindness upon Elymas the sorcerer. It is seen again in Acts 20.7–12 where the young man, named Eutychus, fell from a height and was killed. Paul ministered to him by the working of miracles (so I believe) and restored him once again to life.

Prophecy: This gift is the supernatural ability to speak spontaneously and without premeditation, a special message from God. It is quite different from the gift of prophecy in Romans 12 that we saw was inspired preaching. Here the person who manifests this gift may have none of the qualities or qualifications of a preacher, yet speaks out simply and clearly the word which the Lord has given him.

Discerning of spirits: The gift of discerning of spirits is the supernatural ability which God gives to certain of His people to discern the motivation behind any unusual event or manifestation. There are, in the main, three sources of motivation underlying human events and activities. One flows from

44

the Holy Spirit, another from the human spirit, and yet another from Satan himself. This gift enables a believer to pinpoint the exact source of any statement or manifestation, thus protecting the Church from counterfeits of Satan. We see this gift operating in Paul in Acts 16.16–18 when followed by a slave girl who had a 'spirit of divination'. What she said was perfectly true. 'These men are the servants of the Most High God' but Paul discerned the source of that statement was Satanic. He then proceeded to cast out the evil spirit and protect the work of God from chaos and confusion.

Tongues: The gift of tongues is not linguistic ability, or a special ability given by God to learn a foreign language, but a supernatural utterance in a language never learned by the speaker. It is in fact a manifestation of the Spirit through human speech organs. There is little corporate value in this gift when used in a service unless accompanied by an interpretation, as it will be meaningless to those who are gathered.

Interpretation of tongues: This gift is the supernatural ability given by God to interpret a message that has been given in another tongue. Notice it is an 'interpretation' not a 'translation'. In other words the person who interprets gives the *meaning* of the message and not necessarily an exact translation.

Many Bible teachers and commentators believe

these gifts in 1 Corinthians 12 to be duplicates of other gifts described in the New Testament. One commentator says, for example: 'The "utterance of knowledge; and the utterance of wisdom" described in 1 Corinthians 12 is another way of describing the teaching gift which Paul later refers to in Ephesians 4.11.' In my view that is a mis-statement of the situation. The gifts in 1 Corinthians 12 can operate and function alongside the gifts in Romans 12 and Ephesians 4, but they are quite distinct and separate in themselves, and operate under the control and administration of the Holy Spirit.

Once we lose sight of the fact that these gifts are supernatural in origin and operate and function miraculously under the control and direction of the Holy Spirit, we miss one of the greatest and most exciting truths of Holy Scripture. Some Christians veer away from anything to do with the super-natural. But what if we siphoned off from the Acts of the Apostles, for example, the supernatural ele-ments in it – what would we have left? No tongues of fire! No lame man leaping for joy! No shaking of the building in which the church prayed! No pierc-ing of the hearts of the two who attempted to deceive the Church leaders! No opening of prison doors! Indeed take away the supernatural from the book of Acts (or any other part of the Bible) and you have little left. To emphasise the supernatural does not mean that we automatically devalue human learning, education or personal skills. God uses these, too. However, such are the demands made upon the Christian church that we cannot possibly hope to meet them all unless we have access to God's supernatural and miraculous power.

Let me return now to the experience I described earlier when I set about the task of discovering my basic gifts. Once I saw that God had given me certain basic gifts I then pondered this list in 1 Corinthians 12 and asked myself: 'How do these gifts relate to me?' I saw that just as God had provided me with basic abilities to do certain things well within the compass of His Church, He had also provided me, through the ministry of the Holy Spirit, with supernatural gifts that could expand and enlarge my ministry to an even greater degree than I imagined possible. I saw also that just as God had sovereignly placed within me certain basic gifts, now the Holy Spirit sovereignly wanted to supply me with the supernatural gifts which would add greatly to my effectiveness in His Body. I began to do what Paul advised, and earnestly sought the Holy Spirit for Him to express them in my life. Within months I noticed an amazing thing taking place. Having discovered that my own basic gifts were threefold: preaching, teaching and stimulating the faith of others (or personal counselling) I began to notice that as I pursued these ministries there were times when I became conscious of some of the

47

gifts listed in 1 Corinthians 12 being present in my life. For example, when preaching I found myself also expressing the gift of prophecy. Things I had never prepared to say flowed out from my lips and it was these things that seemed to stick in people's minds long after the rest of the sermon had been forgotten. I found, too, when counselling, that I would say to people such things as these: 'Did such and such a thing happen to you when you were twelve years of age?' or 'What significance do you attach to the fact that when you were eight you were sexually assaulted?' Time and time again I found myself confronting people with events I had no knowledge of and I began to realise in due course that this was the operation of the gift of the word of knowledge at work within me.

The potential for each one of our ministries when wrapped around by the supernaturalism of the Holy Spirit is beyond all telling. Once we discover our basic gifts the whole spectrum of the Spirit is open and available to us so that we can enlarge and extend our basic ministries in the Body of Christ and move forward in the direction in which God wants us to go. Many Christians, I believe attempt to force God to move in the direction they want to go, rather than first finding His basic purposes for their lives, then abandoning themselves to His purposes so that He is free to think in them, love in them and act in them the way He sees best.

5

The gifts of Christ – gifts some become

Having examined the basic gifts described by Paul in Romans 12 and also the gifts of the Spirit listed in 1 Corinthians 12, it is time now to focus on the gifts of the ascended Christ as seen in Ephesians 4.11–12. 'And he (Christ) gave some apostles, prophets, evangelists, pastors and teachers for the perfecting of the saints, for the work of the ministry, for the edifying of the body of Christ.' (AV)

These five gifts are, I believe, gifted *people* who are taken by Christ and placed in His Church to accomplish specific tasks and purposes. They function in the following manner:

1. *Apostle:* The word 'apostle' comes from a Greek word meaning 'to send'. An apostle, therefore, has a strong sense of *mission*. Some believe that the gift of apostleship was a temporary one designed mainly to establish the Church in the first few decades following the death and resurrection of Christ and when this was achieved the work and

role of an apostle was no longer needed. There can be no doubt that the Twelve who were with Jesus played an unrepeatable role in the establishing of the Christian church, but to conclude from that that the gift of apostleship was itself temporary is to confuse the facts. Although the New Testament speaks of the Twelve as apostles in a special sense, it describes many others as apostles also. In 1 Corinthians 15 Paul differentiates between 'the twelve' (v.5) and 'all the apostles' (v.7). In Galatians 1.19 and 2.9, James, the Lord's brother, is described as an apostle, yet he was not one of the Lord's disciples. (See John 7.5). In Acts 14.14 and 1 Corinthians 9.5–6 Barnabas is described as an apostle. There are many other scriptures, which I do not have the space to go into here, that show many beside the Twelve exercised the gift of apostleship. But the question may be asked: 'Is the ministry of apostleship a continuing ministry and is it in existence today?' I believe it is. The strongest argument for a continuing ministry of apostleship is the fact that the Scripture says this and the other four ministries in Ephesians 4 are to exist in the Church *until* we all reach unity of faith. Has that objective been reached?

What then is an 'apostle' and how does he function in the Christian Church? An apostle is a person gifted by God to establish a local community of believers and assist them in laying a strong Scriptural foundation. Ideally he should be 'sent out' from a church or fellowship for this express purpose, so that his ministry can be prayerfully and carefully followed. Unfortunately, many local churches in existence today have never been properly established. They came into existence as the result of an evangelistic crusade, or through a group of believers meeting together to form a local church, but because there was no ministry of apostleship present they either disintegrated or became ineffective in their structure and witness. Denominationalism I believe greatly hinders the ministry of apostleship in today's Church. There are apostles in all the evangelical denominations, who ought, in my view, to be moving through the whole church in general, giving local churches and fellowships the benefit of their ministries, but because they stay within their denominational structures the whole Body of Christ is somewhat deprived. Many local churches need to be re-established, that is to say, they need the ministry of an apostle to come in, restructure the fellowship and help them establish clear goals for the way ahead. The day is not far distant, I believe, when, as denominationalism crumbles, we shall see apostles at work in the Body of Christ in a way we have not witnessed for centuries.

2. *Prophet:* The ministry of a prophet is that of elevating the spiritual vision of the Church, to keep it up to date and to enable God's people to focus on

the goals that currently God has for them. In the *Authorised Version* the word 'prophet' appears in all three streams of gifts. It is found in Romans 12, 1 Corinthians 12 and Ephesians 4. Does this mean they are one and the same gift? No. In Romans 12, the gift (as we saw) is an inner motivation toward preaching. In Corinthians 12 it is a supernatural endowment of the Spirit by which He gives to a person the ability to speak out an unprepared word – a word for the moment. In Ephesians 4 the ascended Christ is seen as taking hold of certain individuals and fitting them into His Church with a ministry such as I have described in the definition above. Having experience of the gift of prophecy as described in 1 Corinthians 12 does not make a person a prophet in the sense of Ephesians 4. The one is a gift that functions in a local community, the other is an office which functions in a wider capacity than a local church. A prophet ideally should be moving through the whole Christian community in sharing his vision, focussing the eyes of the Body of Christ in his area (or indeed the nation) on the goals that God has for His people at that particular time.

The main burden of a prophet's ministry is with the days immediately ahead. His predictions and conclusions, however, must always be consistent with God's written Word, the Bible, and they must always be accurate. The Scripture says 'When a prophet speaks in the name of the Lord, if the thing does not come about or come true, that is the thing which the Lord has not spoken. The prophet has spoken of it presumptuously: you shall not be afraid of him' (Deut. 18.22).

A prophet is an organ of divine revelation to whom the word of the Lord is revealed. Usually the word lies in the heart of a prophet for some time before it is given, during which period the word truly becomes 'flesh' in him. A prophet is not simply a communicator of words, as is someone speaking by the gift of prophecy, as in 1 Corinthians 12, but experiences the word not only in his mind but in his emotions also. As really as Christ was historically mediated to mankind through the body of Mary when the 'Word became flesh' in her, so is the word of the Lord mystically mediated through the mind, the emotions and the personality of the prophet to Christ's waiting Church. He is thus able to convey not only the Word of the Lord but the *feelings* that underlie the heart of God in the issue. He speaks therefore with feeling – the feeling of God.

3. *Evangelists:* An Evangelist, as listed here, is a person who is able to bring large numbers of people to personal faith in Christ. The first name to spring to mind in this connection is, of course, Billy Graham. Here in the British Isles other men recognised as Evangelists in this sense are David Watson, Dick Saunders, Eric Hutchings, Don Summers,

Don Double, and many more. The men who exercise a proven ministry of bringing large numbers of people to Christ are undoubtedly, in my view, the gifts of Christ to His Church.

It might surprise some to discover that in the other two streams of gifts there is no mention of evangelism. This is because the basic gifts of Romans 12 and supernatural gifts of 1 Corinthians 12 are for the building up of the Body, not for reaching out into the world.

Evangelism in the general sense does not flow from the reception of a specific gift but is the natural instinct of everyone who is committed to Jesus Christ. You don't need a gift to evangelise. It is true that some make more effective communicators of the Gospel because of their temperament, their training or their experience, but every single one of us is required to share our faith with our friends and acquaintances by our lips and our lives. But although every Christian is expected to be an individual witness to the Gospel of our Lord Jesus Christ, God has established in His Body a specific gift so that at certain times the Church can act corporately in sharing its faith with the world in a large meeting specifically organised for that purpose. The Evangelist, it must be seen, is a gift of Christ to the Church and because of this the Church must act corporately in using these men as often as possible in presenting the claims of Christ to the whole community. Happily, whole communities of God's people, irrespective of denominations, are feeling the need to share their faith on a corporate basis, and in order for the world to see a healthy church in action evangelism must be less denominational and more interrelational.

4. *Pastors:* Some claim that the gift of a pastor is to be combined with that of a teacher and that really we ought to be talking about one gift here, not two – a pastor-teacher. The main reasons for this view are twofold (1) Paul designated them both by one definite article and (2) every attempt to distinguish between them in practice has proved impracticable. Although the two ministries are more closely connected than the other three we have considered, I still believe them to be separate offices within the Church. A pastor is a person who guides and guards the flock of God in a local community and gently prods them toward spiritual maturity. In other words, he is a spiritual 'shepherd.' If the Church was functioning as it was designed to function, without denominational structures, then a Pastor would have the spiritual oversight of a number of different groups of believers, working with the leaders of these groups (under-shepherds) to bring the whole community into spiritual maturity and prosperity. I do not see a Pastor as being responsible for one local church but moving freely through a number of churches giving them the benefit of his

spiritual wisdom and advice. A true pastor will see not only the needs of one local fellowship but, by reason of his gift, will be acutely aware of the needs of other believers in the community, and ought to be able to share himself over a fairly wide area so that the whole Christian community benefits from his pastoral gift. It is obvious, of course, that because of our divisions and differences the church has not yet arrived at the place where these ministries can function in the way they should. Happily, however, we are moving closer to this ideal and it will not be long now, I believe, before we arrive there.

5. *Teachers:* A Teacher is a person gifted with the ability to make profound truths simple and has the experience to apply the principles of effective Christian living within the lives of God's people. This ministry is more peripatetic than that of a Pastor and this is why I see a distinction between the two. A Teacher ought to be moving amongst the Body of Christ bringing important spiritual truths to bear upon people's lives and teaching them most importantly how to resolve their problems and live effectively for Jesus Christ. The question may be asked: 'What is the difference between the gift of teaching mentioned in Romans 12 and the gift of a Teacher as recorded in Ephesians 4.11?' The teaching gift in Romans 12 would operate in a local community of believers (such as a house group, a Sunday School

group, a youth group, etc.) where the truths of Scripture are expounded and interpreted as they relate to one's individual life. This ministry goes on in our churches week by week in a beautiful and wonderful way. God's people are taught the basic of the faith by those gifted with the ability to expound and explain the Scriptures. It so happens in church life, however, that problems emerge which need handling by men who have a deep grasp of Biblical principles and are able to resolve those problems by sound systematic and clear teaching. Such a person would, in my view, be a Teacher according to Ephesians 4.11.

Many years ago in South Wales in the community where I was brought up and converted, a serious error crept into the churches which caused much heartache and distress. In almost every local church the matter was discussed by different teachers who, using their insight and experience, tried to resolve the issue on a Biblical basis. This produced more division than before. Eventually, the leaders and ministers in the area decided to call in a well-known Bible teacher who, in everyone's opinion, was a Teacher according to the category of Ephesians 4. Hundreds of Christians gathered together over several nights to listen to him expound the Scriptures on this particular issue that was causing concern. By the time he had finished every single person who attended the series of nightly sessions agreed that they now had the mind of the Lord on the matter. There was an instinctive reaction from the whole audience that we had witnessed the expression of one of Christ's gifts to His Church – a teacher who opened up the Scriptures on a major and vital issue that had baffled even the best minds for many months.

In almost every community of God's people there are major difficulties which crop up from time to time which need the ministry of a Teacher in the Ephesians 4 category to resolve. God wants such Teachers to be moving through His Church (not simply a denomination) to bring health, vitality and understanding to His Body, so that, in turn, the Body can present a unified and not a fragmented message to the world.

At the risk of being classified as 'chauvinistic' I believe that the five ministries spoken of in Ephesians 4 are men. This is the pattern of the New Testament and this is the pattern I believe God wants us to follow. I believe that both men and women can operate and express all the ministries in Romans 12 and 1 Corinthians 12 but the enabling and sustaining ministries listed in Ephesians 4 are those of gifted men whom Christ gives to His Body. If it be objected that in the New Testament we read, for example, of women being prophets, then I would say they were prophets in the sense of Romans 12 or 1 Corinthians 12, but not Prophets in the sense of Ephesians 4.

One question often asked whenever I speak on this subject is this: 'If these three streams of gifts are the sum total of what is needed for the building up of Christ's Body, what about the other ministries in the church, such as deacons, elders, etc?' These ministries are appointed by men and not by God (see Acts 6:3). This is not to say that God is not interested in the selection of deacons or elders, or that He does not involve Himself in their appointments, but He delegates to His Church the responsibility to make these appointments, as they deem it necessary and appropriate. If a local church is sensitive to the issues I have presented in these pages, then before it appoints deacons and elders it would seek first to help the ones concerned to understand their basic gifts, for without a true understanding of this a person could be appointed to an office for which they are not ideal, or indeed suitable.

A person who does not posses the gift of 'serving' would hardly make a suitable deacon and, similarly, a person who lacked the basic gifts of 'ruling', 'teaching' or 'stimulating the faith of others' would hardly make a competent elder.

God's plan is for us to first discover and develop our basic gifts and once this is understood we should then open ourselves to the Holy Spirit so that He might endow us with the supernatural abilities that will best enlarge and amplify our basic gifts. We should never strive to go beyond this realm because if it is Christ's desire to place us in the Church as one of the gifted ministries listed in Ephesians 4, then He will do so without any pushing on our part. Remember gifts always make room for themselves. Our Lord doesn't call many to the privileged position of Ephesians 4. They are, compared to the rest of the ministries in Christ's Body, a minority stream. If it is the Master's purpose to make you an Apostle, a Prophet, an Evangelist, a Pastor, a Teacher, then He will make it plain to all concerned. Nothing, nor anyone, can stop you functioning in the role that Christ has sovereignly purposed for you. If Ephesians 4.11 is where the Lord wants you to be then He will work to overcome every obstacle in your life and will confirm it not only to you but to those in leadership positions in the church or community.

The simple principle is this, when you concentrate on discovering and developing your basic gifts and open your life to the ministry of the Holy Spirit for Him to work in and through you, then the whole Trinity will determine the final outcome of your ministry. If that ministry is to be amongst the ministries of Ephesians 4.11 then God be praised. But if not, then God be praised also. The most important thing is to be what God has designed you to be; nothing less and nothing more. Joy, true joy, comes only from discovering your place in the Body of Christ *and staying in it*.